THE FASTEST DINOSAURS

BY **'DINO' DON LESSEM**

ILLUSTRATIONS BY **JOHN BINDON**

LERNER BOOKS • LONDON • NEW YORK • MINNEAPOLIS

To Peter Lessem, my favourite brother

First published in the United Kingdom in 2009 by
Lerner Books,
Dalton House,
60 Windsor Avenue,
London SW19 2RR

Website address: www.lernerbooks.co.uk

This edition was updated and edited for UK publication by Discovery Books Ltd.,
First Floor, 2 College Street, Ludlow, Shropshire SY8 1AN

Words in **bold type** are explained in the glossary on page 32.

British Library Cataloguing in Publication Data

Lessem, Don
 The fastest dinosaurs. - 2nd ed. - (Meet the dinosaurs)
 1. Dinosaurs - Speed - Juvenile literature 2. Dinosaurs -
Juvenile literature
 I. Title
 567.9

ISBN-13: 978 0 7613 4341 7

Printed in Singapore

TABLE OF CONTENTS

MEET THE FASTEST DINOSAURS

WELCOME, DINOSAUR FANS!

I'm 'Dino' Don. I love all dinosaurs. Everyone knows about giant dinosaurs like *Brachiosaurus*. They could run about as fast as the plants they ate. However, some dinosaurs were very fast runners. Have you heard of these speedy dinosaurs? You'll find out about them here. Have fun!

GALLIMIMUS
Length: 5 metres
Home: central Asia
Time: 70 million years ago

GASPARINISAURA
Length: 80 centimetres
Home: South America
Time: 84 million years ago

MICRORAPTOR
Length: 50 centimetres
Home: Asia
Time: 124 million years ago

ORNITHOMIMUS
Length: 3.5 metres
Home: western North America
Time: 65 million years ago

STRUTHIOMIMUS
Length: 4 metres
Home: western North America
Time: 76 million years ago

TROODON
Length: 2 metres
Home: western North America
Time: 76 million years ago

VELOCIRAPTOR
Length: 2 metres
Home: central Asia
Time: 80 million years ago

THE RACE IS ON

A huge *Tarbosaurus* is closing in on its prey.
The long-legged *Gallimimus* doesn't see the
predator coming. *Tarbosaurus* reaches
out to bite. Finally, *Gallimimus* spots the
hunting dinosaur and turns to run.

Tarbosaurus lunges, but the smaller dinosaur's long legs move quickly. *Gallimimus* darts away. It moves much more quickly than *Tarbosaurus*. In a moment, it is safe again.

THE TIME OF THE FASTEST DINOSAURS

Microraptor

Velociraptor

124 million
years ago

80 million
years ago

Dinosaurs first appeared nearly 230 million years ago. Back then, giant reptiles were the Earth's fiercest animals. These animals had scaly skin. Some dinosaurs did too, but dinosaurs weren't reptiles. Dinosaurs walked on straight legs. Most reptiles have bent legs.

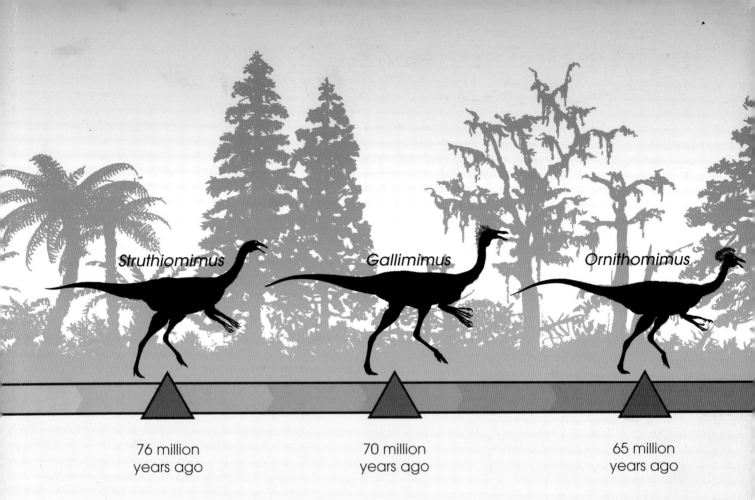

Struthiomimus

Gallimimus

Ornithomimus

76 million
years ago

70 million
years ago

65 million
years ago

Straight legs helped some dinosaurs to run
faster than reptiles. Speed may have
helped these dinosaurs to survive and grow
in numbers. Over time, many giant reptiles
died out. Dinosaurs then ruled the Earth for
more than 160 million years.

DINOSAUR FOSSIL FINDS

The numbers on the map on page 11 show some of the places where people have found fossils of the dinosaurs in this book. You can match each number on the map to the name and picture of the dinosaurs on this page.

1. Gallimimus   2. Gasparinisaura   3. Microraptor   4. Ornithomimus

5. Struthiomimus   6. Troodon   7. Velociraptor

Dinosaurs lived all over the world. Their **fossils** have been found in many places. Fossils are traces left behind by something that lived long ago. Bones, teeth and skin fossils help scientists to think about how dinosaurs might have looked and lived.

Fossils also give us clues about how
dinosaurs cared for their babies. Fossils
have helped us to learn how some dinosaurs
moved from place to place in groups. By
studying fossils, we have worked out how fast
dinosaurs could run.

Fossils of footprints tell us the most about a dinosaur's speed. Scientists measure the distance between the footprints. This distance is called the **stride length.** A long stride length means long, fast legs.

Scientists compare the dinosaur to a living animal. For example, an ostrich is about the same size as some dinosaurs. Scientists take measurements and ask questions. How fast can the ostrich run? What is its stride length? The answers help us to understand how fast some dinosaurs ran.

Bone fossils tell us about speed too. Meat-eating dinosaurs had hollow bones. A hollow bone is filled with air. It weighs less than bones that aren't hollow. The fastest dinosaurs, like this *Ornithomimus*, had light bodies and long, hollow leg bones.

Some dinosaurs were very heavy, like this *Gastonia*. With thick leg bones and plates of armour, these dinosaurs couldn't run fast. Perhaps they couldn't run at all. However, their armour protected them from attack.

REASONS TO RUN

A young *Abelisaurus* on the hunt spots a
little plant eater called *Gasparinisaura*.
She's taking care of her babies in her nest.
She can't run away without leaving the nest.
Will *Abelisaurus* attack her?

Another *Gasparinisaura* darts in front of
the killer dinosaur. The hunter chases him
instead. But *Gasparinisaura* is too quick.
Soon the tired *Abelisaurus* gives up the hunt.

Troodon was the cleverest of all dinosaurs.
It was fast too. This *Troodon* has spotted
a small, rat-like animal. The animal is too
quick for most dinosaurs to catch.

The animal runs towards its hole. It zigzags in
different directions to escape. But *Troodon*
can twist and turn just as quickly. It closes in
on the animal and finally catches it.

A pack of *Velociraptor* dinosaurs is hunting
a young *Pinacosaurus.* The **prey** is only
the size of a sheep. The hunters are even
smaller. They're no bigger than a 10-year
old, but they work together and can run fast.

Speed was very helpful to meat-eating
dinosaurs. They had to be faster than their
prey to catch them. However, *Velociraptor*
had more than speed. Their sharp claws
and team attack made them very deadly.

THE FASTEST OF ALL

In Asia's Gobi Desert, *Gallimimus* are running from a sandstorm. These strange dinosaurs have thin claws and no teeth. They look like fast-running birds called ostriches. In fact, *Gallimimus* and their relatives are known as ostrich dinosaurs.

The ostrich dinosaurs are the fastest of all
dinosaurs. *Gallimimus* are so fast that they
will be able to outrun the sandstorm and get to
safety. Many slower dinosaurs will not escape.

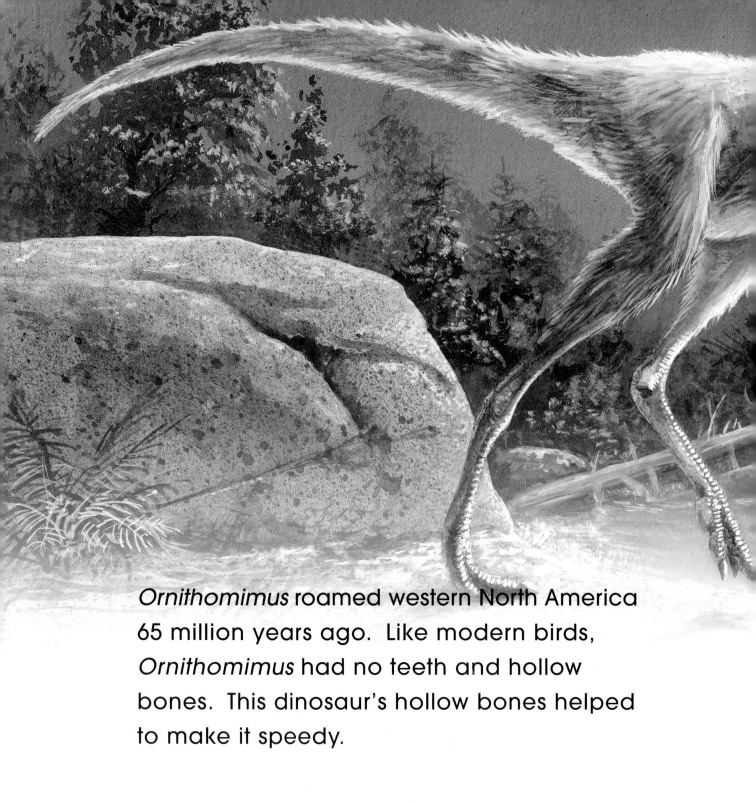

Ornithomimus roamed western North America
65 million years ago. Like modern birds,
Ornithomimus had no teeth and hollow
bones. This dinosaur's hollow bones helped
to make it speedy.

Scientists think that *Ornithomimus* chased
and ate tiny creatures, such as lizards,
mammals and insects. It snapped up these
meals with its toothless beak. This baby
Ornithomimus is about to catch a moth.

A flooding river is washing over the land.
Animals are running for their lives. One
of them is more likely to make it to high
ground. It is *Struthiomimus.* This fast ostrich
dinosaur is very long.

Struthiomimus was built for speed. It was
one of the fastest dinosaurs of all. How fast
was it? Scientists think that it may have
reached speeds of 100 kilometres (60 miles)
an hour. That's much faster than a human
can run. It's even faster than a horse.

THE END?

Many scientists think that a huge rock from space hit the Earth about 65 million years ago. The crash would have raised clouds of dust and smoke. Dinosaurs could have run away from the clouds, but even the fastest could not have escaped.

That's because the clouds would have changed the Earth's weather. Many scientists think that those changes wiped out all the dinosaurs.

Long before this time, many fast dinosaurs travelled the Earth. Some, like these tiny *Microraptor*, had feathers. Feathers helped keep small dinosaurs warm. Some scientists think that feathers also helped some dinosaurs to move around.

Microraptor's feathers and speed might have helped it take off and fly. If that is true, the fastest dinosaurs may not be gone for good. Over time, they may have changed and become the animals we know as birds!

GLOSSARY

fossils: the remains, tracks or traces of something that lived long ago

mammals: animals that feed their babies milk and have hair on their bodies

predator: an animal that hunts and eats other animals

prey: an animal that other animals hunt and eat

stride length: the distance between an animal's footprints

INDEX